CROSS SCHOOL LIBRARY

ANIMAL POEMS

Valerie Worth

Pictures by Steve Jenkins

FARRAR STRAUS GIROUX

NEW YORK

Distributed in Canada by Douglas & McIntyre Ltd.
Color separations by Chroma Graphics PTE Ltd.
Printed and bound in China by South China Printing Co. Ltd.
Designed by Robbin Gourley and Véronique Lefèvre-Sweet
First edition, 2007
10 9 8 7 6 5 4 3 2

www.fsgkidsbooks.com

Library of Congress Cataloging-in-Publication Data
Worth, Valerie.
Animal poems / Valerie Worth ; pictures by Steve Jenkins.—1st ed.
p. cm.
ISBN-13: 978-0-374-38057-1
ISBN-10: 0-374-38057-0
1. Animals—Juvenile poetry. 2. Children's poetry, American. I. Jenkins, Steve, ill. II. Title.

PS3573.O697 A82 2006
811'.54—dc22

2005056812

For our grandchildren
—G.W.B.

For my father
—S.J.

SNAIL

Only compare
Our kitchens
And bedrooms,
Our lamps and
Rugs and chairs,

To the bare
Stone spiral
Of his one
Unlighted
Stairwell.

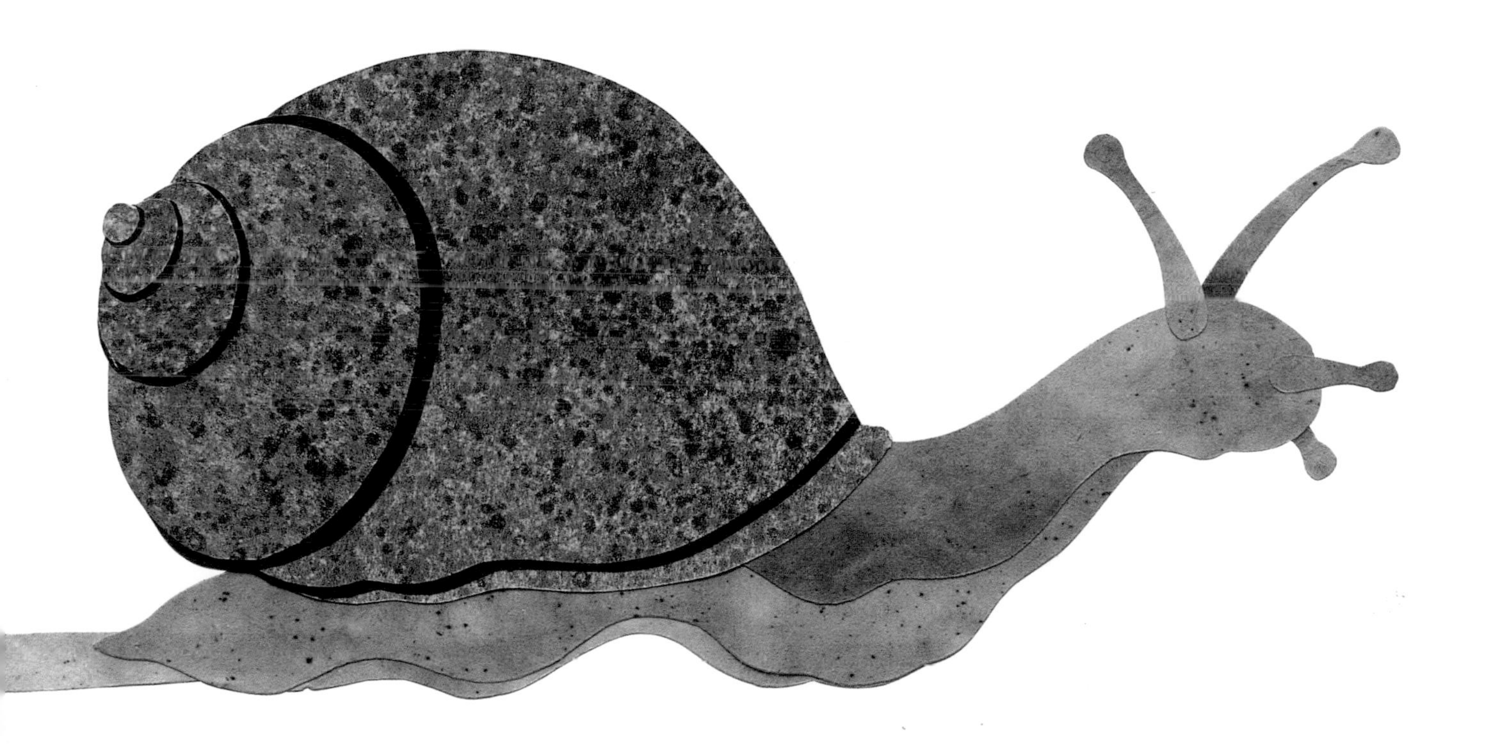

WHALE

Too heavy to live
On land, where only
Winged things escape
The weight of stones,

His whole hill of
Flesh floats easily
In the sea, light as
Dust in sun-baths

Or earth balanced
Buoyant in thin space—
Every gravity, whether
Gnat, atom, or planet,

Made, like the whale,
To fit where it is
Found; poised perfectly
In its own place.

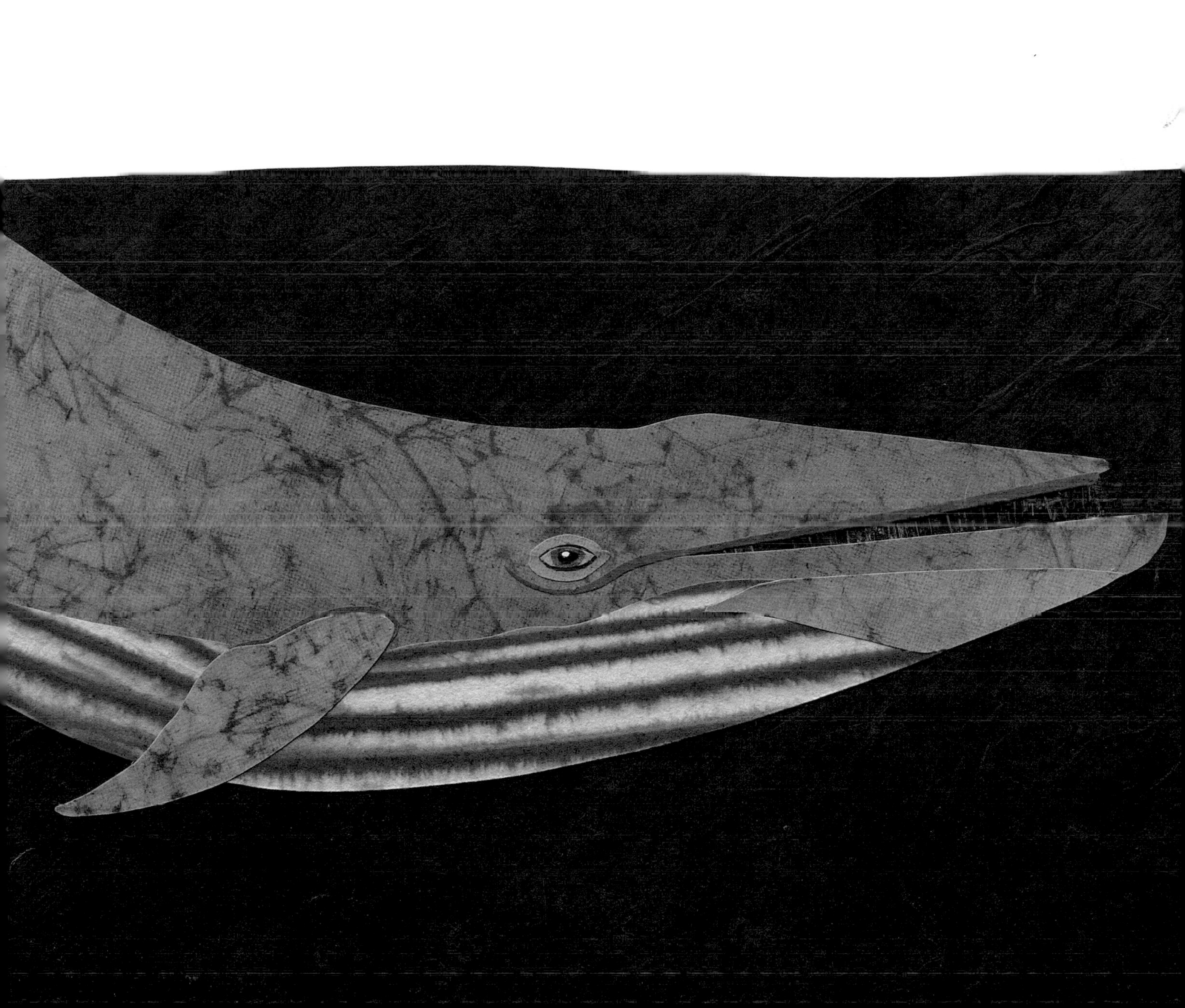

BAT

The bat sees
Only in the dark
Side of earth,
Taking dust and
Clay for his
Colors, holding
Aloof from
The gaudy sun;

He cleaves to
The cave roof
Like a grim
Flake of flint,
Or flings out
Like a surly
Stone thrown
After the sun:

Knowing no better
Than hardheaded
Earth does,
That in his
Own blind
Veins run
The lighthearted lavas
Of the sun.

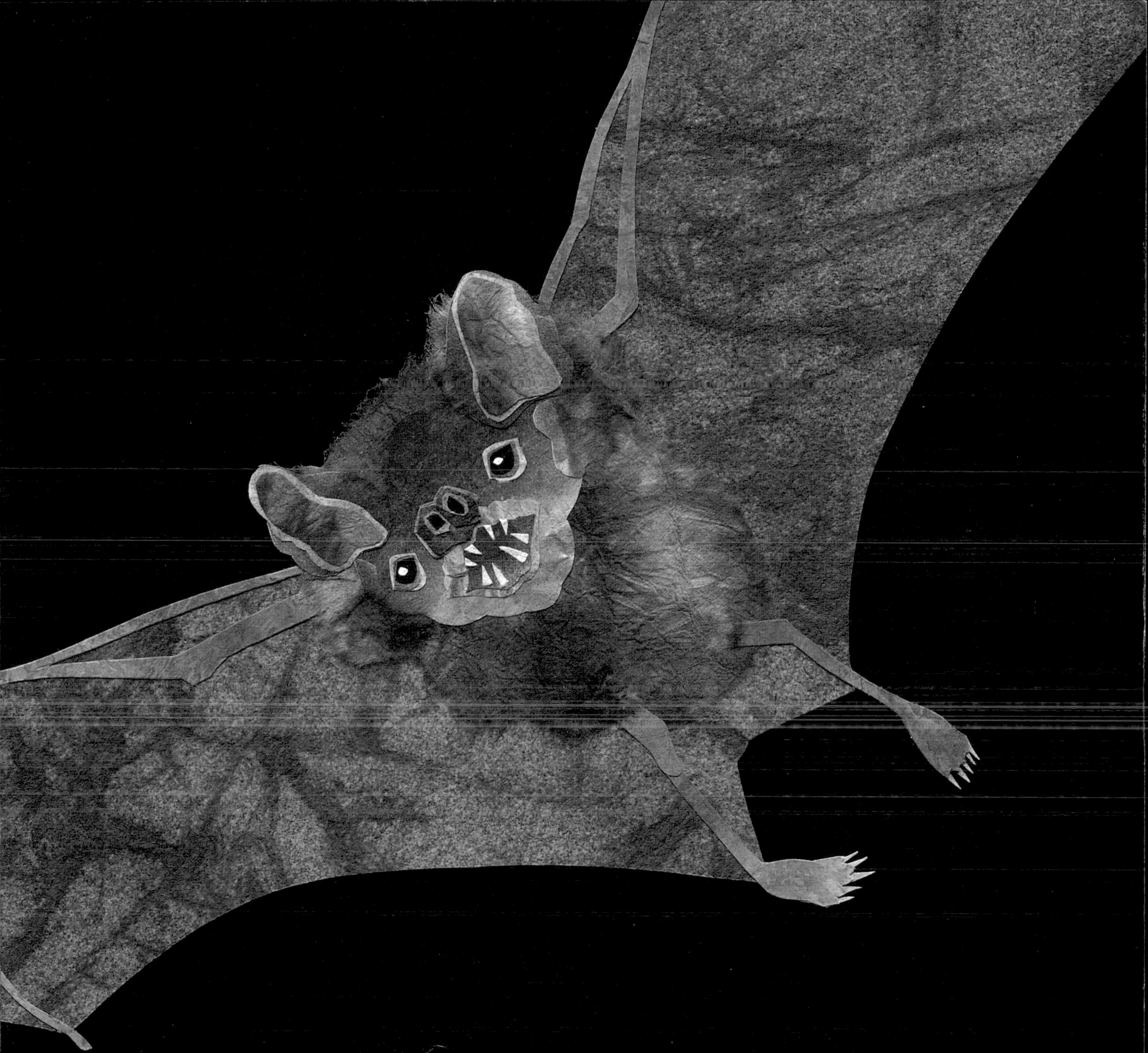

GROUNDHOG

Not my shadow
I dislike,

But that sad
Sunlight

Creeping so
Weak across

The winter-
Weary snow:

Who wouldn't go
Back to bed

And sleep until
The sluggish sun

Starts wide-awake,
Clambers out,

Shakes his
Dusty fur,

And gambols
Away glad

Through the
New grass?

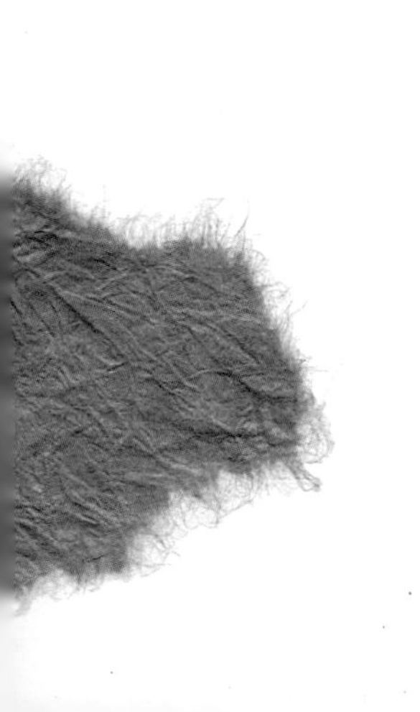

CAMELS

They can afford to be ugly
And ungainly, to stand
About munching and belching
Like smug old maids

Remembering their ancient
Sway, when bearded
Traders sailed them over
The starry sand-waves,

High-laden with baled
Silks and spices, with
Camphor and indigo, amber
And amethyst and gold—

All hidden away now
In their dusty humps,
As precious waters hoarded
Against dry days.

PENGUIN

Where the only
Land is ice, loose
Crystals worked
To white diamond
By ridge heaped
Upon crevasse, or
Carved into looming
Emerald veins, or
Pressed past sapphire
To the shuddering cobalt
Gloom of the berg's
Abysmal bone,

The penguin swims
At home, or frolics
Over the treacherous
Floe; or amidst
Those fearful frozen
Smolderings, settles
To its nest of
Snow: cheerful
As a house cat
Toasting its haunches
On the hearth's
Warm stones.

SQUIRREL

Late autumn rains
Fall colder than snow,
When the wet wind's floods
Wash down from the trees
Their last ragged leaves—
Except where the creaking forks
Of the high black boughs hold fast
These rough brown bundles, woven so deep
Not a drop nor a draft may seep
Inside, to the nest where
The gray squirrel sleeps:
Wrapped snug in his fat,
And his fur, and the curl
Of his tail.

WASP

Like a dark
Flame flickering
At the puddle's
Muddy rim,

Gathering a single
Dab, gone,
Glittering back
For more,

She is sprightly
And dangerous
In her ornamental
Blue-black bone—

She is a
Sharp flake of
Night, let loose
In daylight,

A dab of dull
Earth, grown
Lively and deadly
As the sun.

ELEPHANT

The elephant
Consents to curl
Her trunk on
Command, to stand
On a tub,
And other foolish
Tricks that are
Part of her job;

But when it is time
For the tent
To move to another
Town, she
Is the only one
Who can pull
The tall
Poles down.

MINNOWS

No minnow
Swims alone—

Though the dim
Brown kind

May weave a
Single figure

With its school
Of muddy fellows

As they dash
Among the shallows,

While the glisteners
That shine

Through aquarium
Shadows

Seem to follow
One another

Through a measure
So fine

That their slivers
Sift together

In a scintillating
Mesh,

A smooth-
Linked flesh,

Like the whole
Rushing shimmer

Of a solid
Silver fish.

SNAKE

Loosed
From
Limbs to
Run like
Water,
Spilled to
A liquid
Silt, a
Slurry
Of scales,
Grain after
Grain
Lapped
Into a
Single
Cataract,
Gathered
To one
Glazed
Stream
Of latticed
Panes, or
Mottled
Mosaic
Of pebbles
Tumbled
Smoothly along,
Their slender
Landslide
Filing
Down
The narrow
Channel
Grooved by
The guiding
Head,
Poised
A little
Aloft,
Wearing
A bed
In the air
For the
Following body to

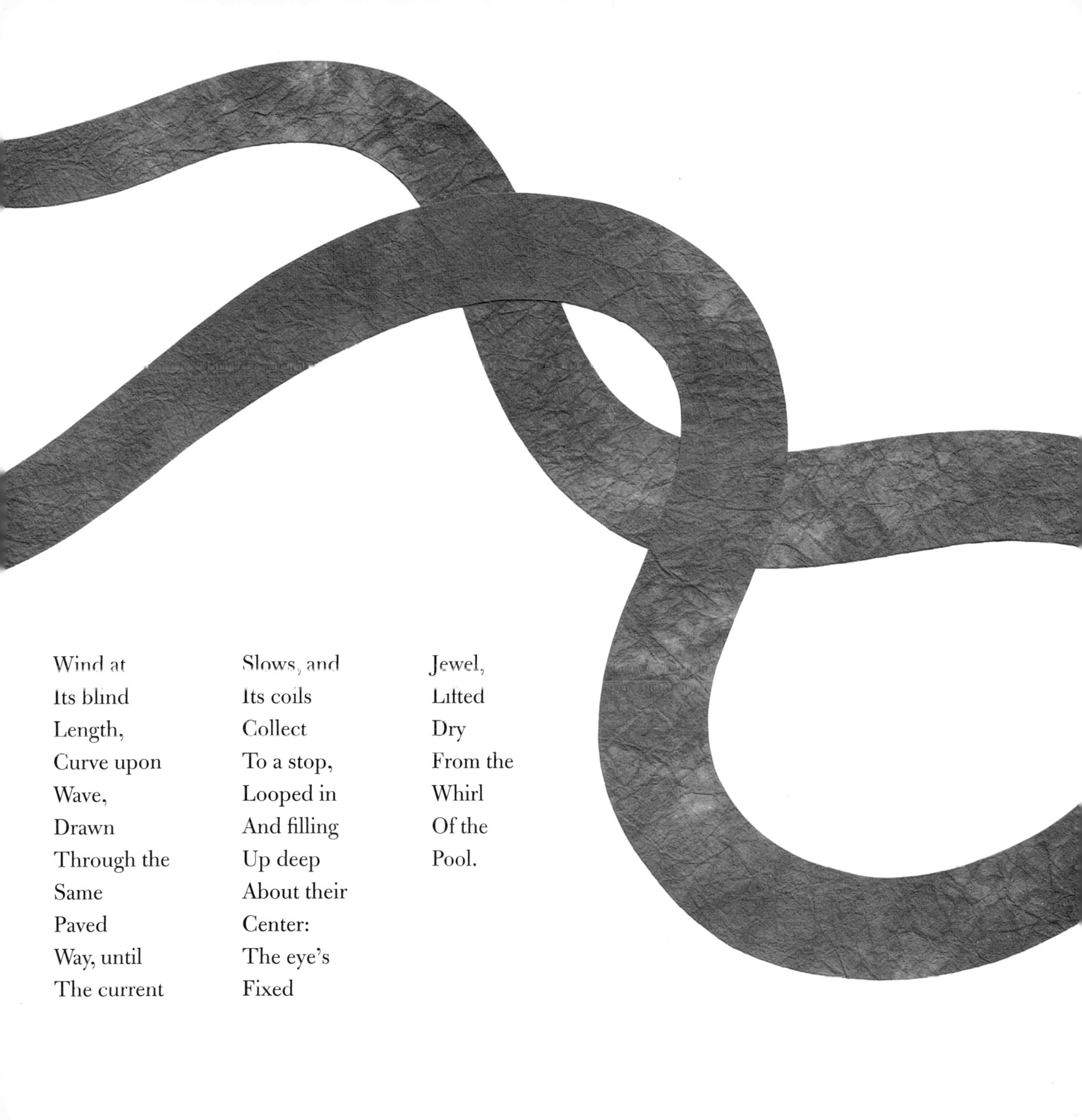

Wind at
Its blind
Length,
Curve upon
Wave,
Drawn
Through the
Same
Paved
Way, until
The current
Slows, and
Its coils
Collect
To a stop,
Looped in
And filling
Up deep
About their
Center:
The eye's
Fixed
Jewel,
Lifted
Dry
From the
Whirl
Of the
Pool.

HUMMINGBIRD

Most creatures
Came the long
Way, through
Slow earth,

But the quick
Hummingbird
Sprang straight
From the sun,

Or flew
Like a spark
From the
Earliest star—

Even now
Aflicker with
The first
Struck light;

Even now
Awhirr with
The dark's
Atomic thrum.

KANGAROOS

The trouble is,
Once born, there's
No going back—

Except for these
Babies, who can
Leap about free

Until they've had
Enough; and then by
A simple somersault

Return headfirst
To the delectable
Pocket of the dark.

BEAR

The bear's fur
Is gentle but
His eye is not:

It burns our
Way, while
He walks right

And left, back
And forth, before
Us: he

Looks, and we
Look, and his
Hot eye

Stings out
From the dark hive
Of his head

Like a fierce
Furious
Bee.

PORCUPINE

Held fast
In the thicket
Of its own
Thorns, the
Porcupine's
Timid body
Blooms safe
And alone,
Unruffled,
Unharmed;

But in
The warm
Disarming
Weather of
Spring, doesn't
It long
To flower
Out of that
Cold bower
Of spines,

And fly
With the
Blithe petals
Of mice
And hares,
Scattered
Across the
Silky
Perilous
Meadows?

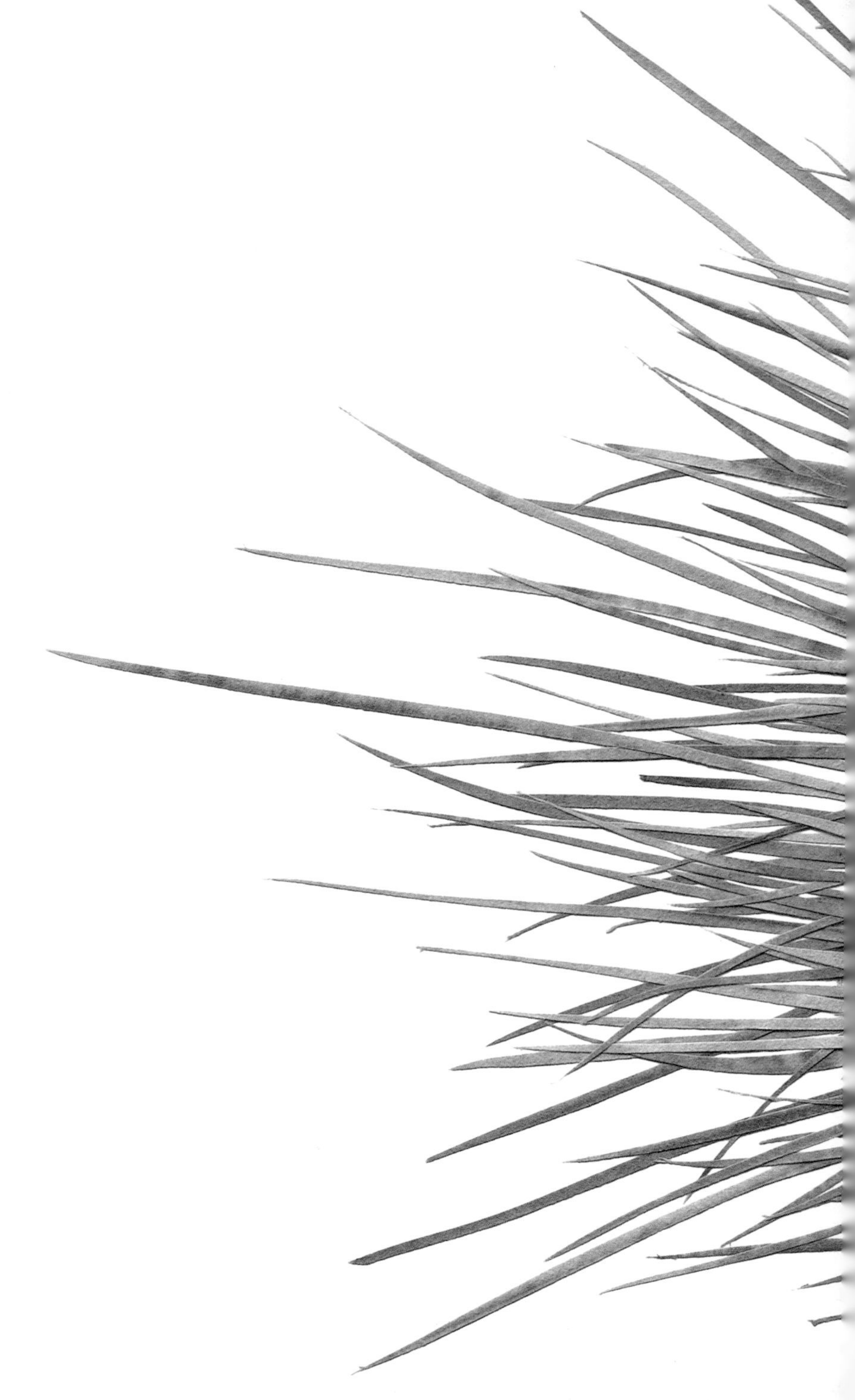

JELLYFISH

Rising under water
Like transparent
Ghost-bells
Of lost lands,
Their hollow
Veils and
Trailed clappers
Peal eternal
Knells, for
Valleys drowned
And flooded hills
Where only the
Slow conch strolls;
Swung in the
Sighing swell
They lean and
Toll, until,
Washed ashore,
Their glassy
Domes collapse
And sink away
To silent tears,
Wrung dry
Upon the sand.

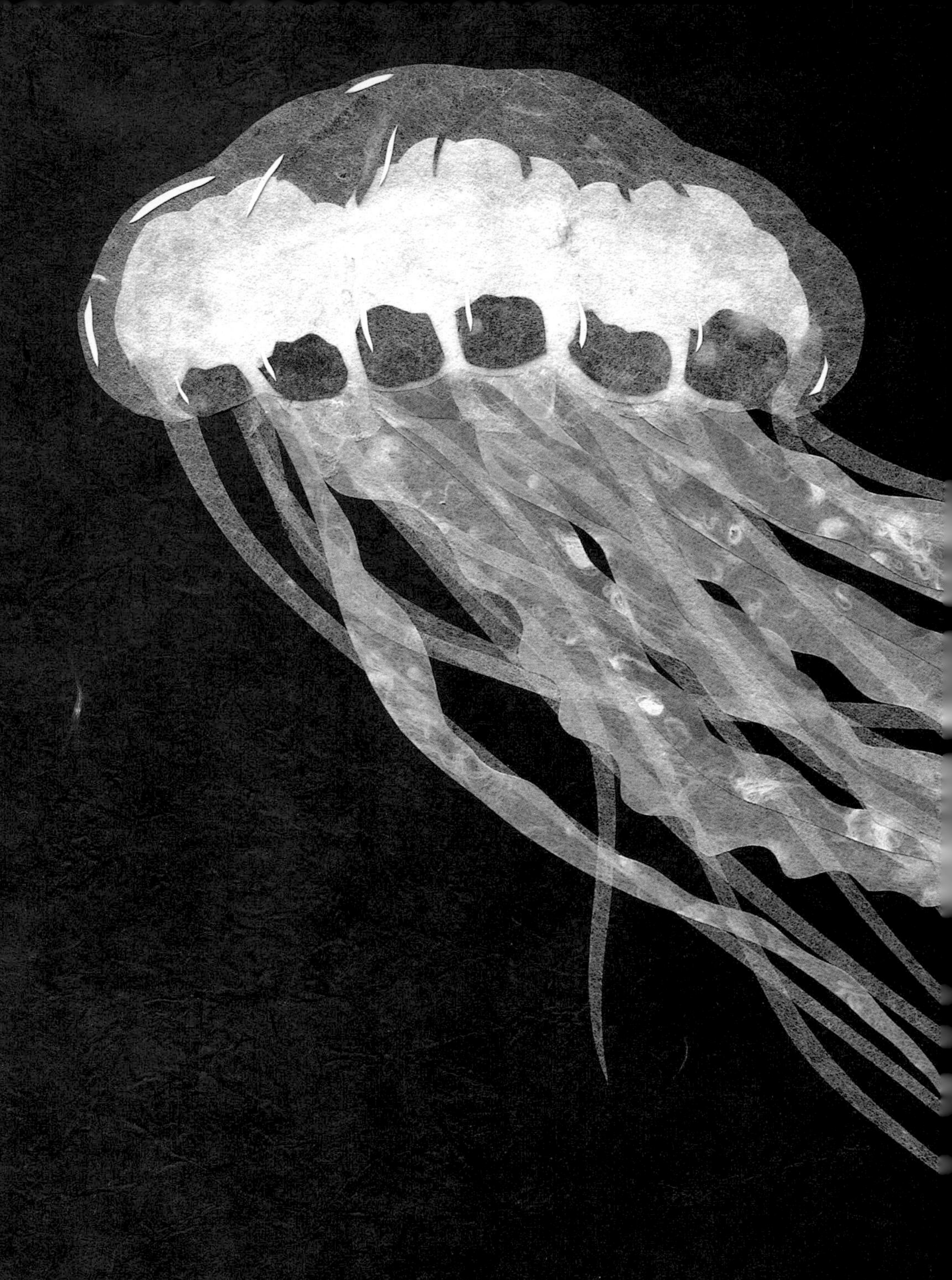

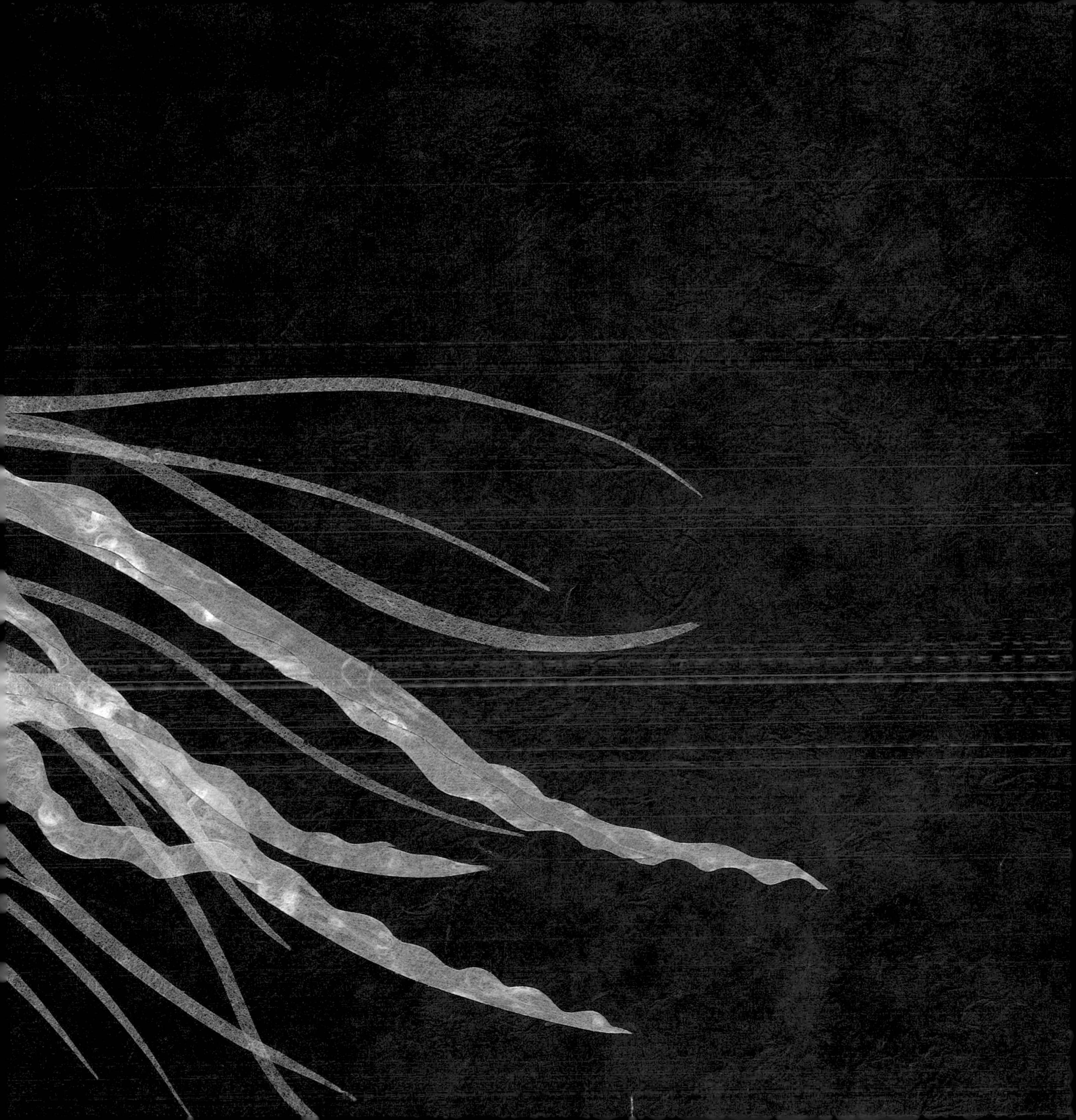

WREN

As though a stray
Leaf, fluttering over
The grass
Before the wind,

Were picked up
On some different
Gust, shaken
And spun

And dissolved
To a strange
Spiral spirit
Of dust,

And then cast
Out, reborn
In the form
Of a wren—

The exact bird-
Shape, yet
Left
Resembling

That brown-curled leaf,
And still remembering,
Unreconciled;
Even so finely

Netted into the
Flutter and flirt
Of the wren,
Still fretted with

Its other tree-
Life: always
Skittering back,
Twig to twig,

After some lost
Site or scar
To grasp, and be
Itself again.

GORILLA

It's not just
Awe that
Draws us
Near, to
Stare through
The bars
And exclaim
At that
Glaring
Legendary
Ogre
Of rough
Black iron
And ebony,
But also
Jealousy:
As we
Might have
Stayed
Or become
The same—
Strong
Enough to
Fear no
Enemy;
Feeding
Serenely
On celery.

COCKROACH

Of the many creatures
That wriggle and creep
And make some people
Shudder, I don't mind
Snakes or mice or
Caterpillars or worms—

Though I don't quite
Care for ants—but
One that I can't
In the least abide
Is the cockroach: not
So much that it scuttles

And bristles, and glues
Its slippery eggs in
The cracks of books, but
That it looks so clever:
As though it knows
My particular horror,

And plots to stalk
And startle me better—
Today I dart from
Behind the sugar, tomorrow
I skulk in her sneaker
And twiddle her toes . . .

OWL

The owl
Has eyes
For mice

That hide
In the midnight
Grass

Like fiery
Stars
At noon—

Concealed
From all
But the wise.

RABBITS

The wild brown
Rabbit leads a
Shabby life, dogged
By fever and
Famine and fleas,

Even when it's not
Frozen with fear
To a furred clod,
A clawed stump,
An eyed stone;

While the spoiled
Pet bunny lolls
In a careless
Daze, a slumped
Satin pillow

Stuffed with
Lettuce and ease,
Left little to do
But groom its limp
Unlistening ears.

STAR-NOSED MOLES

Shovel-pawed,
Pick-clawed,
Snouted with stars
For lamps to
Lead them keen
Along unlighted
Shafts, the moles
Fatten their
Fortunes mining
The common soil:

Tunneling shallow
Clay to put
Their portly way
Among the roots
Of grass—where
Succulent insect-
Nuggets shine,
And worms unwind
Their sumptuous
Veins of ore:

Luxurious fare,
And proper to
Those velvet-coated
Appetites, their taste
For treasure fed
On all the buried
Wealth of earth:
The golden beetle-
Grub, the silver
Eggs of ants.

SPIDER

The spider weaves it,
Swinging and switching
Her thread, running it
Round its frame,
Closing the last flat
Spaces in, to wait out
Her purpose of flies;

But at dawn, when
It hangs spangled
With silver water, frail
Crystals of wet light
Caught so neatly and
Needlessly, it is not
Her web, but ours.